Two hearts entwined in eternal dance,
Bound by love, not by chance.

In her eyes, he sees his tomorrow,
In his smile, she forgets all sorrow.
Hand in hand, they step into the light,
Their love shining, oh so bright.

Today is a beginning, a page so new,
An anthem of love, pure and true.
In the sacred echo of the wedding bell,
A timeless tale, they begin to tell.

Mermaid

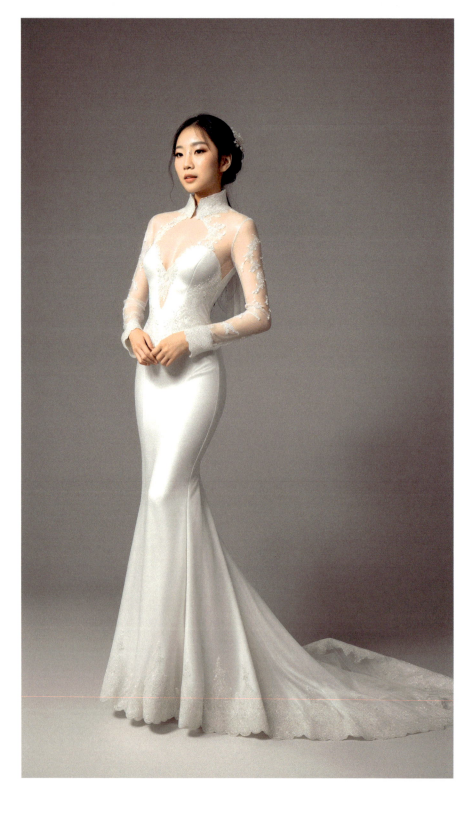

Ballgown

Jumpsuit

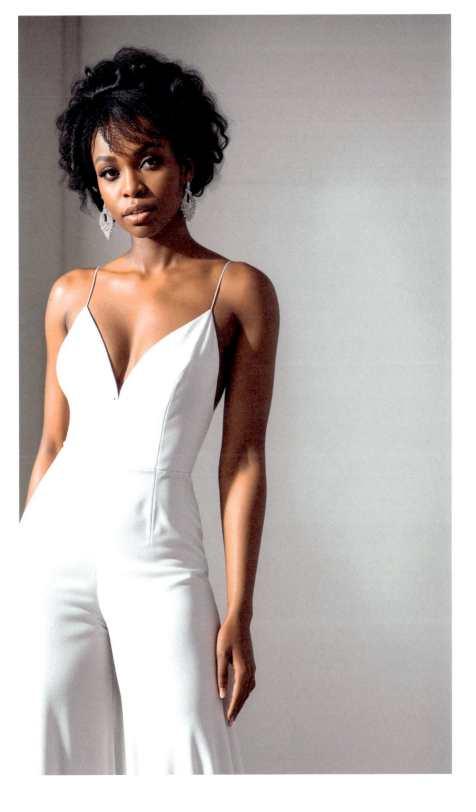

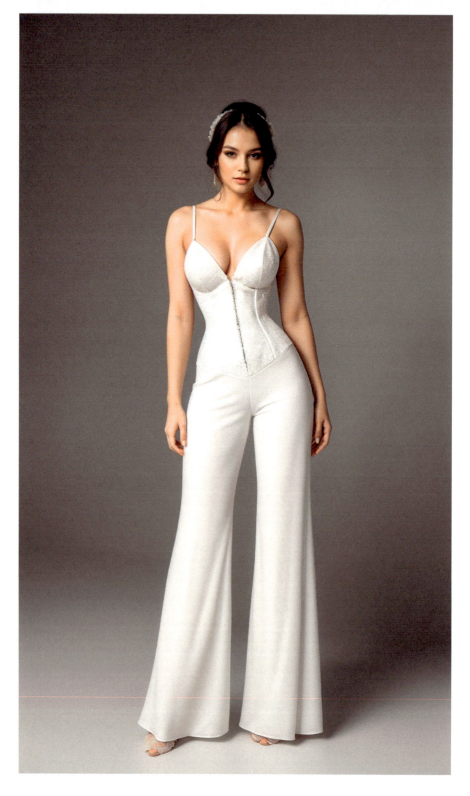

Short Dress

Plus Size

Made in the USA
Columbia, SC
01 April 2025